Every finger... what we cannot do, God in us can do.
What seems impossible to us is possible only with
God–The Miracle Engineer.
A book full of innocence, love and faith,
these experiences of a young boy with God, will touch
your soul and offer inspiration and hope.

The
Miracle Engineer

*A young boy's day-to-day miraculous
experiences with God*

SACHIN THOBDE

New Age Books

ISBN: 81-7822-274-4

First Edition: Delhi, 2005

© 2005 by Sachin Thobde

Published by
NEW AGE BOOKS
A-44 Naraina Phase-I
New Delhi-110 028 (INDIA)
Email: nab@vsnl.in
Website: www.newagebooksindia.com

Printed in India
at Shri Jainendra Press
A-45 Naraina Phase-I, New Delhi-110 028

*God's want for your happiness is deeper
than your own want for it.*
— CYRUS HOSHI MERCHANT

Contents

❖

REGARDING GRATITUDE

A WORD OF CAUTION

Acknowledgements

Thank you God, thank you very much for helping me, guiding me, showing the path and for your unconditional love, abundant grace and really thanks for making everything possible.

Thank you everybody at New Age Books, thank you very much for your cooperation and support. I thank Mr. J.P. Jain, my editor Anand Sir and Kavita madam.

Thank you Mummy Rajashree Thobde and Daddy Chandrakant Thobde for moral support.

Thanks to all the writers especially Iyanla Vanzant, Cyrus Hoshi Merchant, Og Mandino, Dr. Brian Wiess and others whose names surface in the book, for their writings, I got immense guidance after reading them.

Introduction

God and Angels

❖

*"The things which are impossible with
men are possible with God... ."*

– Jesus

Miracles happen every single day. Yes, they do.
The Miracle Engineer, our Best buddy God is aware
of every single thought in us. And as we speak our
heart out to Him, He shows up. Even if you don't
He still is around us. Said, unsaid prayers, spoken,
unspoken wishes and requests are all granted to
us. You think about a thing you want and all of a
sudden it appears before you, you don't have to
go towards it, put any effort to get it, it itself comes
towards you. This all is true because of God's
immense, endless and unconditional love. We
receive all the miracles and receive his blessings
every single day. Absolutely no coincidences.

Which miracle machine keeps working, I don't know. I guess it is called 'Celestial Sweetheart.' Yes sweetheart of God and angels and all of us. His beloved children and all of this again belong to 'Celestial Sweetheart Co. Unltd.' In other words this Kingdom of God is liable for doing all the good things, miracles, blessings, supreme benedictions and for our joyful, peaceful, beautiful and wonderful life. How does God read our every single thought, may be because as we speak our heart out to Him the SMS's are directly sent to God and Angels, from your heart to the heart of God and Angels, heart to heart, absolutely no networking problems and as soon as they receive the SMS's (short messages sent), they send their SMS's (sweet messages sanctioned). Sometimes they'd put you on hold for sometime but there is nothing to worry as hold on simply means "You are worth it but we have worthier plans for you."

"How" a miracle happens is again a miracle from the Miracle Engineer. Just have faith, faith is not just a word or a thought, faith means "God is at work." However, when we don't have faith, it doesn't mean God is not at work but His work is doubled. Firstly, He will have to free our mind, but don't worry, ever freeing our mind will also be done by way of miracles and blessings. So you just have faith, trust, patience and obey the word of God and enjoy all the miracles, blessings from God for us all and our loved ones every single day.

I thank God a lot for His immense help, love, support, blessings and miracles and I have realized that my thank you notes will never ever be enough for Him.

Now when you'd read the book and get into the pattern of experiencing miracles and blessings from Him every single day, you too will realize that our buddy God, dear Miracle Engineer does too many things for us, our thank you notes will never ever be enough for Him.

MIRACLES HAPPEN
EVERY SINGLE DAY

One

A God Sung Musical Miracle

❖

"God has created the world in play.... It is God himself who is sporting in the form of man... ."
— Ramakrishna

My favorite song is 'Allah Ke Bande Hans De, Jo Bhi Ho Kal Fir Ayega.' If explained by words it means "Get a smile on your face because Heaven's are going to fill your heart with their Celestial Love very soon." Or else one can also say "Just have faith in God because to God all things are possible."

Now this song really has a beautiful meaning behind it, thanks to the lyrics by Vishal and it was released in September'03. So on 31st December'03 or on 1st January'04 at around 0:01 after wishing everybody a happy new year at home I decided to listen to this song on my walkman. But just before switching my walkman on, I tuned to radio station GO 92.5 FM to see how they are celebrating the new year. And lo! a miracle, a Grand miracle.

The people who had sung this song, i.e., singer Kailash Kher and musicians Vishal-Shekhar were present in the radio station and played the song 'Allah Ke Bande Hans De' live.

Now just when I am about to listen to this particular song on my walkman simultaneously the real singers and musicians are there in the radio station and playing the most beautiful song live at 0:01on 1st January'04.

I just felt as if God is playing that song in Heaven's radio station and practically telling me that just have faith in Me because Heavens are going to fill your heart very soon.

This is the best, grandest and most beautiful miracle and since then miracles have just been following. So after that if I would ever feel bad about something I would just remind myself what God had told me on 1st January'04. Remember a little faith and the Heavens are going to fill your heart with their Celestial Love.

Two

The Miracle of Footprints

"To me every hour of the light and dark is a miracle, every cubic inch of space is a miracle...."
    – Walt Whitman

Then there was another grand miracle which I'd received from the Miracle Engineer.

In June '02, I was in 12th grade and I was alienated from God. Though I had hundreds of reasons to, but just in a short while His immense love unfolded and I was a transformed person. Now I know for sure His love is endless for me and for all of us.

Besides not studying regularly, I never did disobey His word, but I was not regular in studies. In the 12th grade I just didn't bother studying. The

12th grade exams which are held by university added worries on me as I was not prepared for them. Rather I expected the result to be very poor. I gave my university exams in March'03 and in June'03 I got the results. My maths paper had gone really bad and I expected nothing more than 55-60 marks. But sometimes I did wonder what it would be like getting 55-60 marks in maths.

I'd got 33/100 in maths in my college preliminary exams and in my university exams I got 88/100. The explanation to this high raise of marks from nowhere is completely inexplicable. Only because of God's love and therefore just a beautiful miracle. The marks which I didn't expect to come came from 'nowhere' which according to Iyanla Vanzant is God's spiritual location that leads to 'now here'. Yes folks here I was receiving the marks from 'nowhere' coming straight into my marksheet as 88 and making it 'Now Here.'

With this my percentage also soared up to 74% in the 12th grade in commerce field. And then when I was experiencing all miracles from God and as God was trying really hard to get me close to Him, yes me close to Him, because as Janina Gomes has said, "God is closer to us than the air we breathe" I did start feeling His immense love for me.

The next day I went to my cousin's place to show my marksheet and as we were sitting in the hallroom there was one bookmark which read the following lovely story.

Footprints

One night a man had a dream. He dreamed he was walking along the beach with the Lord. Across the sky flashed scenes from his life. For each scene, he noticed two sets of footprints in the sand; one belonging to him and the other to the Lord.

When the last scene of his life flashed before him, He looked back at the footprints in the sand. He noticed that many times along the path of his life there was only one set of footprints. He also noticed that it happened at the very lowest and saddest times of his life.

This really bothered him and he questioned the Lord about it. "Lord, you said that once I decided to follow you, you'd walk with me all the way. But I have noticed that during the most troublesome times in my life, there is only one set of footprints. I don't understand why when I needed you the most you would leave me."

The Lord replied, "My precious, precious child, I love you and I would never leave you alone. During your times of trial and suffering, when you see only one set of footprints, it was then that I carried you."

–Author unknown

It was then that I realized and experienced the real faith of God who helps us so much and does carry us during our times of trial.

Anyway, as I told you I still don't know how I got 88/100 but it only shows God's immense grace and unconditional love towards us and yes, "During your times of trial and suffering when you saw only one set of footprints, it was then that I carried you." Thank You God.

Three

The Miracle of Extra
Thirteen Days

❖

*"Miracles only happen to people
who believe in them...."*

— Anonymous

Now to become a complete Chartered Accountant
you have to clear 3 examinations, Professional
Examination(PE)-1, PE-2, PE-3. I was appearing for
PE-1. CA exams are held all over India twice a year
in May and November and on the same date and at
the same time. Till today CA exams have never been
postponed, but once there was some problem and
at that time they were preponed.

Now even after receiving my results of the 12th
grade in June'03 I still had my CA exams in May'04

and even by Feb'04, I hadn't been serious with my studies, I didn't even have proper notes of all the four subjects. But I was gaining immense faith in God and was very very happy with it. I used to tell my college friend Jovel Rodriguez all about the Glory of God and how He is performing miracles and how He keeps helping me all the time. Then I told him that my CA exams are set for May'04 and I'd better get serious with studies, as there was little time, I also told him that now I'd just put in my best and to Him leave the rest. And then a miracle.

Did I say that CA exams have never been postponed? But this year in May'04 they were postponed for the first time. The day I told Jovel about my studies and CA exams and how little time was left with, the same evening I got a call from him saying that, there is some news going on the news channel about the postponement of the CA exams. And yes they were postponed by thirteen days—instead of 8th May'04 they were scheduled on 21st May'04. Now an extra time of thirteen days in CA exams is really a big bonus. Exams were postponed on account of elections being held in the country. And even if the date of voting in my state was prior to 8th May, in other states the dates clashed with the date of my CA exams and as they are held at the same time all over India they had to be postponed.

Now I didn't even ask God to help me or give me extra time but He understood my problem and right on the day in the morning when I told Jovel about all this, evening I get a call from him saying, "CA exams all over India have been postponed." Postponed for the first time. I just thanked God for performing another of his Grand miracle and helping me again.

Four

A Cute Little Miracle

❖

"There are only two ways to live your life. One is as though nothing is a miracle. The other is as though everything is a miracle...."

–Albert Einstein

During April–May'04, when I was preparing for my CA exams, initially for three continuous days I studied quite well the subject of mathematics and on the third day while I was studying, I reached a saturation point when all of a sudden this thought came to my mind about asking for some relaxation from the Miracle Engineer. And so I said, "Ok God I am really tired so miracle....just send some miracle."

Now I don't know how so quickly, but yes it did

happen that I was sitting at home and studying in my room at the sixth floor of my building and right from the fourth floor of the opposite building someone played this song "It's the time to disco."

This is a Hindi song from a Hindi feature film 'Kal Ho Na Ho' and only two or three lines of this song are in English. I just don't know how, but after I'd told the Miracle Engineer to do something, some relaxation for my mind, within a fraction of a second this song started playing and the most fascinating thing was that, the first line of this song is "We just dancing" and after two to three lines, it goes on to say "It's the time to disco" and that was the first line I'd heard, in a fraction of a second, after telling the Miracle Engineer to perform some cute little miracle for me.

I again felt very happy. But unfortunately it wasn't the real time for me to disco, as my CA exams were approaching in two-three weeks.

Five

A B E A Utiful Miracle

❖

"Faith is a simple childlike belief in a divine Friend who solves all problems that come to us...."
– Helen Keller

In India we have the private cable operator system and my cable operator puts four movies a day; Hindi movies during morning and afternoon hrs. and English movies during evening and night hrs. The evening show starts at around 5:30 p.m.

Now one day as I was really getting bored, around 5:25 p.m. I switched on the TV. I've by now developed a good appetite for movies with a lot of drama like *Beautiful Mind, Forrest Gump* or movies like *The Passion of the Christ, City of Angels.* I wanted the cable operator to put some really good drama or movie regarding God, based on God. But then I was wondering which other, not too old a movie, would rather be there based on God or a drama. I'd already seen the above mentioned movies four to five times. So I just said in my mind, "God put some good movie, I am getting bored, so even the one's which I've seen four to five times would do." And you know what, the Miracle Engineer came to my rescue again. Again He perfomed a beautiful miracle.

Did I say that I asked for a drama or a movie regarding God or based on God? And you know which movie the Miracle Engineer put up .... 'Bruce Almighty.' I've seen the movie three to four times but at that moment I couldn't recollect this particular movie regarding God or based on God.

Just five minutes. before I'd spoken my heart out "I am bored", "put some good movie regarding You" and He did put some beautiful movie regarding himself—'Bruce Almighty.'

Again I was very happy as the tiniest request is granted in the tiniest span of time, i.e., in less than five minutes. and of course, I did get a few laughs on my face after watching Jim Carrey, fortunately for a while, becoming the Almighty.

A B E A Utiful miracle.

Six

A Sunny Miracle

❖

*"Things of God that are marvellous are to be
believed on a principle of faith, and not to be
pried into by reason...."*

– Samuel Gregory

There was heavy rainfall in the latter half of July'04
and we at Mumbai, India hadn't seen the sun for
around two weeks. Black clouds and showers all
the time. So everyday while going to college I never
did forget to wear my windcheater.

One day while I was getting ready to go to
college, as usual, I kept reminding myself that I
don't have to forget to wear my windcheater. But
any how I forgot to wear it. Now I don't know why
on this particular day that I forgot to wear my

windcheater. It was only when I reached the bus stop that I suddenly realized this lapse on my part.

The Miracle Engineer again had planned it beautifully; showers for a long time, the sun disappears, all waiting to see the sun, then on one beautiful day, I forget to wear my windcheater and just when I am about to decide whether to go home and get my windcheater or not, my gaze goes straight up into the 'Bright Blue Sky' and miraculously, quite miraculously I see the 'Sun Shining High.' This miracle again, was really very beautiful.

Seven

The Miracle of Delay

❖

"Faith does nothing alone—nothing of itself, but everything under God, by God, through God...."
– John Stoughton

Right now in July'04, I am studying in the Narsee Monjee College of Commerce and Economics. Now this college is quite far off from my home and to reach the college I have either to take a bus or a train. I leave at around 7:00 a.m. and take a bus which starts exactly from the entrance of my building and stops exactly at the entrance of my college. If I take a train then I have to get off on the station. The station is at a distance from my college. So while coming to the college I prefer a bus and while going back home I prefer a train, don't mind walking till the station while going back home because if I take a bus at around 11:30 a.m. there is heavy rush on the road and so the bus takes approximately 30 minutes more time than the train.

Bennett Matthews is my good friend and he stays very near to the college. So for him to come to the college and to go back home, it just takes about 10 minutes by bus.

Its simple, I take a bus to reach the college but while coming back home I travel by train and Bennett travels both ways by bus.

I met Bennett in my first year of college in June'01 and we became good friends because both of us liked reading books. We used to spend a lot of time talking about this book, that book, this book into movie and that movie into that book and blah! blah! blah. But now in June'04 we are in the fourth year of our college and after the first year we have never been in the same class because of the shuffling of our college divisions. But we used to meet each other quite often as we were in the same college. And now I really wanted to meet him and tell him all about God, Divine books etc. I even tried his contact number but couldn't get through him.

On 7th July while I was attending lectures I'd got tired and didn't want to attend the last lecture which was at 10:45 upto 11:35 a.m. and so I wanted to go home. But just as the previous lecture got over the professor of the next lecture came in. There was no way but to attend that particular lecture. While she was teaching I said to myself, "God, I wanted to go home. Now I have to wait till this lecture gets over, another 50minutes." But then I thought maybe this delay is for some good reason, may be God again has some miracle to show to me.

And then after the lecture got over, when I left and came down, I met Bennett. I wanted to tell him everything about God and His miracles, about the books, but as I told you Bennett takes a bus to go home, the bus stop is exactly at the entrance of our college and I have to walk till the station.

But because of that miraculous delay I'd met Bennett and miraculously on that day Bennett had some kind of work, because of which he too had to go towards the station. I told him as much possible as I could and when we reached the station, miraculously I realized that it was the 7th of July and the following day the 8th of July, which is Bennett's birthday. So all of a sudden I wished him, though in advance, "Happy Birthday Bennett."

Again the Miracle Engineer had performed it beautifully; delay because of that lecture, I keep the faith (I know for a very small reason but I like living life this way), then out of the blue I meet Bennett, meet him after gap of about six months, then he too for some particular reason wants to come upto the station and the best of all after reaching the station, after telling him about God and his glories, God miraculously reminds me that tomorrow is his birthday.

Eight

The Miracle of 'Faith' 'Size of a Mustard Seed'

❖

"If you have faith as a grain of a mustard seed,
you shall say unto the mountain,
'Remove hence to yonder place,'
and it shall remove and nothing will be
impossible to you...."

– Jesus

Now I'd heard of this famous quote "If you have faith size of a mustard seed... ." but I didn't know it completely. So I thought I'll type in the internet search engine and find out what the whole quote is and what does it signify.

But on that day I noticed that my right side

wisdom tooth was coming down in a little bit crooked manner. My gums were hurting very badly, just for a day though, but for a day, yes they were.

So I had to go to the dentist. I had been to the same doctor some 5 to 6 years ago for some cavity fillings and I do very well remember, those two days of cavity fillings! I had the time of my life.

My dentist is a very humble person, a complete gentleman, but a dentist. So when I imagined myself sitting on the dentist chair I got a little bit tense, my teeth had to go through the same old drilling and all of that. But again I kept the faith. Again I thought "Whatever happens, happens for the best." And the next day I went to the dentist.

An unbelievable miracle, really unbelievable happened there. I was waiting outside as there was one patient before me and one patient after me. A few magazines were kept on the corner table. So I took one of them but I don't remember its name. I don't remember whether the magazine was regarding political issues, traveling, automobiles or something else. I only remember that there was this three-page story regarding "The Mustards."

I didn't even recollect that yesterday I'd decided to lookout for the faith quote in the search engine. But as I was reading the story there was something written about the famous quote, "If you have faith, size of a mustard, you will say to this mountain, remove hence to yonder place and it will move and nothing will be impossible for you."

I just couldn't believe another of our beautiful, wonderful Miracle Engineer's grand miracle. Yesterday was the day when I thought I'd find out the faith quote in the internet search engine, then I get the tooth problem, I go to the dentist, I blindly keep walking in my faith and by which magic miracle machine on God's green planet earth do I find the faith quote in a dentist dispensary's pass time magazine! Miraculously unbelievable.

To tell you the truth I'd gone partly insane at that particular moment. I was looking here and there and thinking and wondering. I just couldn't believe how these miracles keep happening every single day. The other patient who was sitting in front of me started wondering what's wrong with this guy and you know what, after I came out from the dentist's cabin and saw that guy, he too had started reading the same magazine and must have wondered what treasure did I find in there.

Anyway all these miracles bring unlimited joy to my life. One important thing we must remember dear reader is whatever things may seem to be, like going to the dentist to trim my tooth or a delay or anything else, when you walk with faith, the size of a mustard seed, you'll realize how the Miracle Engineer performs another of His unbelievable miracles. And then don't forget to express your gratitude to the Miracle Engineer, a thank you to our dearest buddy God.

Nine

The Miracle of Books

❖

"God alone is good and perfect...."
– Anandamayee Ma

Books are your best friend. They truly are. You may or may not have any other friends but books are and will always remain your best friends.

When I faced any problem and tried to explain to someone, they would tell me what to do or what not to do, or whether I was wrong or someone else was wrong. Nobody ever told me to go to God and take it easy, just have faith and trust God and everything will be all right, no one ever spoke about God anytime.

That's ok because the Miracle Engineer, He Himself told me about Him. He is the One who helped me know Him. It was He who got me closer to Him because he is already closer than the air we breathe. It is He who has willed all the beautiful things for us, all miracles, all supreme benedictions, peacefulness, joyfulness, fun, happiness, a pleasant, delightful, beautiful, wonderful life. And the only reason behind He willing so much for us is His immense, unlimited, unconditional love towards all of us.

Now how did He help me to know Him or get close to Him is firstly because of his endless love and secondly by way of books. Books have articulated Him very well. The Miracle Engineer, our dear buddy God has helped people articulate Him very well. I started reading Cyrus Merchant's 'Forever The Faith,' 'Heartfelt' and 'Welcome Back To Life.' And I liked them a lot because life seemed to be different after that.

So I wanted to know more of these self-help books. I wanted to read more of His books, I wanted to know more about Him, wanted to know more of God's glory for us and how His Kingdom is working 24/7 to make our life glorious. But other authors, other books, which ones to read? Now just to know the name of authors and their books, there came another cute little miracle.

The next day I picked up Cyrus Merchant's 'Welcome Back To life' and believe me some Angel might have really held my fingers, because I opened the book to the exact page. This is what I found on it. 'Welcome Back To life' page no.117

But first pick up the books: 'One day my soul just opened up' and 'Yesterday I cried' by Iyanla Vanzant, 'Autobiography of a Yogi', 'Divine Guidance' by Doreen Virtue, 'Beloved' by Toni Morrison, 'A course in miracles' and everything by Og Mandino. Then there is Sarah Ban Breathnach, Brian Wiess, Marianne Williamson, Kahlil Gibran, Mary Baker Eddy, Gary Zukav and all the Chicken soup for the soul and most of the self-help. They are worth it.

Yes I was very happy to see this again. I am not even asking God to do anything but He has already read my mind and answered beautifully. Thank You again dear buddy God, M.E.

Self-help books are really very helpful for God has helped me immensely by way of books and extravagantly and modestly by His own Beautiful ways. I know He loves and takes care of you in the same way; Immensely, Extravagantly and Modestly. You too dear reader, read books exploring the glory of God. And then when we live out our life with complete FAITH, OBEDIENCE, TRUST, BELIEF, PATIENCE we realize that books have really helped and God, Angels and His Kingdom are very beautiful, wonderful and most of all we realize that

Their love for us is fabulously beyond the grasp of our own understanding.

You will start actualizing your beautiful, wonderful life as you will come to know the infinite love of God for us and how unlimited additions are made to the supernormal happiness of our life everyday. And then please don't forget to spread the word around.

Ten

The Miracle of a Decade

❖

"God is concealed from the mind
but revealed in the heart...."
– Anonymous

Every week either on Tuesday or Wednesday Cyrus
Merchant writes a column called 'Heartfelt' for our
local newspaper Bombay Times, The Times of
India. But in July'04 I noticed that his column had
not featured since 2 to 3 weeks which means no
Heartfelt column twice or thrice. So I was thinking
why were Cyrus's articles not coming in the
newspaper? One Tuesday ok, but twice or thrice?

So then while I was praying I requested God, "God
why aren't his articles coming in the newspaper? Just
take care of him. See that he is alright."

I prayed on Wednesday night and for the first time his article appeared in the Thursday edition with the title 'End of a Decade.' He had completed ten years of writing his Heartfelt column.

I thanked God again for answering my prayer and again the Miracle Engineer had spoken beautifully.

Oh Thank You dear buddy M.E.

Eleven

The Miracle after the Prayer of all the Living Creatures

❖

"When people are loving, brave, truthful, charitable, God is present...."
– Harold Kushner

"Let us be Gods and then help others to be Gods...."
– Vivekananda

I cannot recall who wrote, "If you do pray for the peace of all mankind, then why only for the peace of all mankind, why not for the peace of all the living creatures."

Previously before going to bed I used to pray to God, "God let your love heal all the errors and let there be only one expression of love." Though unknowingly I'd never included any living creatures in my prayers besides human beings. But after taking Mr.Anonymous's advice into account I did include all the living creatures in my prayers. And you know what, then again a sweet little miracle.

This movie 'Cats & dogs' was released in 2001 and after my praying to the Almighty for the well-being of all the living creatures, just one or two days later when I switched on the TV this is what I saw on it. First I saw the trailor and then,

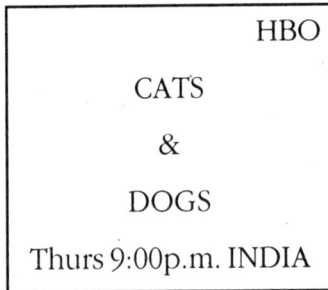

```
                              HBO

            CATS

              &

            DOGS

       Thurs 9:00p.m. INDIA
```

All of this, life with God, goes on so meticulously perfect. When you pray for yourself, very beautifully God sends some miracles and your prayers are answered beautifully. When you pray for others, very beautifully God sends some miracles for them and again your prayers are answered beautifully. When you pray for the well-being of all the living creatures, God in a way sends some kind of a miracle "Cats & Dogs—Thursday 9:00p.m. on HBO" and again your prayers are answered beautifully.

Thank You God.

Twelve

The Miracle of God's Real Passion

❖

"There is not in the world a kind of life more sweet and delightful than that of a continual walk with God. Those only can comprehend it who practice and experience it...."

–Brother Lawrence

The movie 'The Passion of the Christ' was released in India somewhere in May'04 and I wanted to watch this movie. But my CA exams got over on 25th May. So I thought I'll sit at home for a while and when they will release the movie on CD I'll watch it. I didn't want to go to the theater and all. And then I thought if I would go to the theatre, whom would I go with, I didn't want to go alone. My best friend Jovel Rodriguez had already seen that movie and because of the tight schedule of his courses he didn't have the time for a movie.

But on the next day one of my other college friends, Juzer Dalal called up out of the blue and as our vacations were on and the theatre was very close to his home, asked me to accompany him to watch the movie 'The Passion of the Christ.' Initially I showed my reluctance as I needed some rest after my CA exams. But on his persistance I went to see this movie the next day.

Now just on one particular day I had been thinking about this movie 'The Passion of the Christ.' But then I also thought whom to go out with, but again it was 'The Passion of the Christ.' So I thought I'll wait for the CD and on the next day, out of the blue, I got a call from my old friend who stays very near to the theatre. It is as if God sends some company, as if God doesn't want me to wait for the CD, as if God forces me to watch the movie even if I feel I'm tired and think that I'll watch it later.

The Miracle Engineer had already read my mind without my even saying anything to Him. He understands it, understands all of us, sends some company and forces me to watch 'The Passion of the Christ.' Oh thank you God and I do know for sure what your Real Passion is like for all of us.

Thirteen

The Miracle of Cloud No. 309

❖

"Love is the nature of God, He can do no other: thus to be God, love at each moment...."

– Angelus Silesius

Now Virender Sehwag is our very good (hitter) cricketer in our Indian cricket team. In January'04 he went abroad, scored 195 runs in a test match, went to hit a six and got caught and so was out on 195 runs.

After that series he came to India and got engaged to his girl.

Now in April'04 he again went abroad and scored 295 runs in another test match and went to hit a six. This time it went all the way and he got his 301 mark and was out on 309.

Then he came back to his home country India and got married.

It simply says that when things didn't go his way, like a six not on 195, it is just God saying that you are worth it but I have worthier plans for you, so keep pursuing, and that's why a six not on 195 but a little further on 295.

Now see this celestial chain, folks, made by God, our dear buddy Miracle Engineer; goes abroad 195 runs, comes home, gets engaged, goes abroad 309 runs, comes home, gets married.

And this celestial chain is not meant for some of us but for all of us, because He loves all of us equally and we are His Beloved Children. We all have God and our God has Us and that's why life is a never ending Celestial Chain because God's love is Equal, Endless,, Immense, Unlimited, Unconditional towards All of us and so we receive Miracles and blessings every single day.

So when things don't go your way, when there are disappointments, don't think God is denying you. We may sometimes deny God but He, no matter what, never ever denies us. How can your Heavenly Mother, Heavenly Father turn their back on their little Beloved Children. God is just saying, " You are worth cloud no. 9 but I want to take you a little further on CLOUD NO. 309." So you better witness not your cloud no.9, but God's CLOUD NO.

309 for yourselves. And then don't forget to write your unlimited thank you notes to God.

> Life is just like
> God Bless
> Therefore no mess
> Not a test
> Only Rest
> Not just in peace
> But in Zest

Fourteen

The Way to Miracles

❖

*"When you arise in the morning, think of
what a precious privilege it is to enjoy, to love...."*
— Naraus Aurelius

*"If the only prayer you say in your entire life is
"Thank you," that will suffice...."*
— Meister Eckhart

You are also experiencing His miracles everyday.
If you don't think so then simply pray to God. He
has created us, He knows us completely,
understands us perfectly. Start your day, when you
get up early in the morning, by simply saying "God
send some miracles today," "God at this moment I
am getting bored, I need a miracle," "God in this
matter only your Magic can help me out." Then just

live your life. Keep up with all the good activities, don't bother when, how, what Magic Miracle will take place because Miracles are sent out of His Endless Love for us, to celebrate every moment of Our Life. And then when you'd start experiencing miracles every single day of your life you will Thank Him so much and you'd realize that your thank you notes are never enough for Him. Soo much the Miracle Engineer keeps doing for us.

But sorry, sorry if you have lost any of your loved ones, then don't feel sad because wherever they are, they are very, very happy and as Cyrus has said, "Death is not real instead we wake up in the real world, whenever you lose any of your loved ones then you gain your Angel, so gain your Angels now and if you cry for them, they hate to see you unhappy because they are very, very happy." Death is just a part of your life, not the end of life. Life simply goes on beautifully from death into Eternity with your most special Soulmate or Loved Ones together eternally. So now that you know that your Loved ones are much closer to you than the air you breathe, you just have to speak your heart out to them, just ask them to show a sign or give a signal that they are present very much near to you, just beside you and suddenly a glorious miracle will take place. 100%. It was quiet for a while and all of a sudden heavy showers start pouring or the breeze starts blowing swiftly or the sun was covered for a while and all of a sudden it comes out and you get to see the bright shining sunlight. A glorious miracle will take place, everytime when you speak your heart out, a miracle will take place, I know that for sure. Not my promise but God, Angels—your most special loved one's promises.

Your purpose in life is just to party, and the reason to party is you. Life is that simple.

Purpose: to party, reason to party: you. All of this for a small price of 'obedience.' Remember what Mother Teresa has said, "God doesn't require us to succeed, he just requires that you try."

> Obey the word of God
> You be His kid at your best
> To Him leave the rest
> He will keep sending you
> Presents fab much better than the best.

And then you just have to keep on enjoying the enchanting ride of your beautiful life.

Your present becomes very very beautiful, you can undoubtedly see a very, very joyful future and when you reach the future you see the glorious, miraculous memories of the past.

A small price of obedience and miracles will be experienced by you 100%. No matter how hurt you may be feeling, how very bad you may be feeling don't ever give up on God, people do hurt people, for that reason don't ever turn away from God. According to me this has been a very important reason for alienating from God. Go all the more closer to God, He will mend everything for you, He is going to mend everything, all miracles, all blessings a wonderful life, He has willed it for you 100%.

When you feel hurt or angry or tend to get frustrated know that no matter whatever it is, God is always there with you. So just hold on. Be patient, calm down and the most important thing is God is our best friend, God and Angels are our best friends. He created us, we didn't choose to come down here on earth, He chose us, Blessed us with the Invaluable and Eternal Gift of Life. The Heavenly Mother, Heavenly Father. God knows what you are feeling, God deeply understands you, God's eye witnesses everything. As Cyrus Merchant has rightly said, "Nothing escapes the Lord's eye, least of all your tears." Sometimes we tend to misunderstand Him as to why is He letting such things happen to us. He is not. It is people's freewill. But don't worry it is like what someone has rightly said "Nobody is worth your tears and the one who is worth it will never ever make you cry." Nobody has power over you besides God and His Kingdom and they will make use of this power of their love only to take you to a much, much higher pedestal. Only for you to live a beautiful, wonderful and a miraculous life.

Hold on for a while, everything will unfold before you in time. Always remember to surrender it to God.

Everything that happens, happens for the best. I know faith comes after experience and if you are really feeling bad and you have hundreds of reasons to give up on God, please don't ever give up on God, I too did have reasons but always remember the footprint story. Remember that in your darkest hours you can see the brightest stars. This Brightest Star or these Brightest Stars are the Real Light of Your Life. As Confucius has said, "Silence is a true friend that never betrays" and Aldous Huxley, "After silence that which comes to expressing the inexpressible is Music." That's how I think this book was created.

If you ever feel guilty of something then know that no matter what, forgiveness is the result of God's True Love and none of our mistakes are so big that God cannot forgive. If you have any piercing regret, then give up that matter in God's Hands. Always give everything in God's Hands, from our side it should be complete surrender. As Cyrus has said, "Surrendering doesn't mean giving up, it means trusting God to bring into manifestation the very thing you want to have if it is right for you. The weak resign, the strong trust and surrender." He is our Best Buddy, dear Miracle Engineer and Best mender and then you will see how He furnishes, polishes and gives an Enlightening touch to your wonderful life.

God can and most importantly 'Does' help us in ways we can't even imagine. So just PRAY. As Iyanla Vanzant has said, "PRAYER is the Best skill we have and the Best service we can offer to God is again PRAYER." So PRAY, PRAY harder with full confidence and you smell victory.

Today or tomorrow He is going to grant your wishes 100%. So all the time be with God, right from today be in complete alignment and accordance with God, be okay with others and be okay with yourself, Always keep your Self-Respect intact. Nothing is ever worth the price of your Self-Respect. Today or tomorrow He is going to give you everything you want. Don't worry about the patience section. Don't try to figure out how long you will have to wait. As Cyrus has said, "The longer it takes to have your wishes fulfilled, the fuller will be their fulfillment." So if you think it is taking longer than the longest, then the fulfillment will also be fuller than the fullest. And to tell you the Truth, it never ever takes that long and even if it takes a little longer or not, the fulfillment is always fuller than the fullest. ONE HUNDRED PERCENT TRUE.

Why does God do so many things for us "just

because," "just because" He loves us Immensely, Unlimitedly, Endlessly and Unconditionally. That's why I tell you really Thank God, for the gift of life is wonderful, invaluable and eternal, if you don't believe it, oh then very soon you will realize it, witness it for yourselves.

REGARDING GRATITUDE

Fifteen

Thank You God

❖

*"The worship most acceptable to God comes
from a thankful and chearful heart...."*
— Plutarch

*"To create something new, or to keep receiving
more of something you have already gotten,
get some paper and pens and write a
thank you to the Universe...."*
— Sanaya Roman

Thank You God, thank you very, very much for
the invaluable and eternal gift of life.

Now where and how many times can we keep
saying thank you to our best buddy the Miracle
Engineer, God, He shows up everywhere.

He shows up by answering our said, unsaid

prayers, by granting our spoken, unspoken requests. Helps us mend everything, heal everything. He is the best magician and that's why things show up from nowhere and become 'Now Here.' Loves us immensely and unconditionally, helps us, gives us immense support and during our times of trial carries us etc.Etc.ETC. because His love knows no bounds for us.

And as I've been experiencing all miracles from the Miracle Engineer, and if you are not, then I know for sure 100% you are also going to start experiencing them, I used to keep thanking Him all the time and just after thanking Him suddenly some other miracle used to take place. So at that time I used to think how many times should I keep thanking Him? He keeps doing soo much for us and you know what, He even helped me to express my gratitude towards Him. As it is rightly said in the Koran, "Even if you use all the trees as pens and oceans as ink, you wouldn't be able to write enough thank you notes to God."

So when you start experiencing miracles, when you get fab much more than you asked for, and when you know that you always keep receiving His Miracles and blessings every single day, I am sure you too will realize that "Even if we use all the trees as pens and oceans as ink, we wouldn't be able to write enough thank you notes to God."

A WORD OF CAUTION

Sixteen

Yes a Word of Caution, Because

❖

"God's grace is the the oil that fills
the lamp of love...."

–Henry W. Beecher

"God is able to make all grace
abound toward you...."

– New Testament

Think twice before approaching God because "TO
GOD ALL THINGS ARE POSSIBLE." This is actually
an understatement because it says "If you approach
God, All things will be Possible to You, there will
be a Possibility of Everything, you will Possibly have
Everything you want." But the truth is even if you
approach God or do not approach God, out of His
immense sweethearting love 'He is' going to, not

'He will' but 'He is' going to give you everything, all that you want. Today or tomorrow 100% sure. Remember this again, it may take a little longer to get your wishes fulfilled, but fulfillment (God's promise) is always fuller than the fullest (God's love).

So think twice before approaching God, if you haven't approached Him yet because God takes care of you not one or two hrs. a day but for every single moment of your life.

So think twice before approaching God, if you haven't approached Him yet because this is the truth whoever you are, wherever you are, you just belong to one and only one Kingdom of God, i.e., Heaven and that's why I tell you as you belong to His Kingdom you don't get in your life what you can ask for, you only and always get fab much more than you can ever dare to ask for. Think twice before approaching God, life would be so beautiful, so wonderful every moment a miracle, some magic, for some moments you may even lose your sanity. Don't worry to get your sanity back, He will perform another miracle. So think twice before approaching God for you will get soo many things that you won't know what to do with them, you won't know where to keep them.

Oh you doubt it, very good, be thankful for your doubts because very soon you are going to know that your doubts are never real, only some crap false beliefs and so you will be sure that the only true thing is God's Endless and Unconditional Love for you. This is the only Truth and yes the Truth can't be altered or changed and the doubts did make the Truth all the more truer and now that you know the Truth you have the strong zestful, faith filled life.

Yes everything is magic, if you can't figure out something then wait, hold on, everything will unfold to you in just a short while, just a short while and then when the mystery is revealed you'd know what Marianne Williamson has said "No matter what you can ask for, it is just a microscopic view of what God wants to give you." The verse in the previous chapter about gratitude is very, very true. So think twice, your thank you notes are never going to be enough for the Miracle Engineer. We keep receiving His miracles and blessings every single day because of His endless love for all of us. We all belong to that MNC, i.e., Miraculous Nation's Corporation, Heaven and all of us are the Miracle Engineer's, God's beloved children. So think twice before approaching God, this is just a word of caution because then you'd have to make a separate journal consisting only a distinction between what you asked for and **What God Gave You.** So think twice before approaching God for you'd keep on getting soo many things you won't know what to do with

them, you won't know where to keep them.
Until next time, I'd like to conclude with :

THE MIRACLE ENGINEER

Believe or don't believe
You are receiving them on every single day
What are they?
They are miracles to say.

Miraculously He created you
And countless more Miracles He Has kept for You
Those Miracles are coming to You
Not just for today or tomorrow
But for every single day to be true.

He is the Best Magician
And He let those Miracles Happen
To celebrate your life with your loved ones
He is sending you gifts that are made in Heaven

Miracles from the Miracle Engineer
Can get you in a bit of fear
How is life so wonderful
Is the only thing you will wonder!

So be prepared to receive the Miracles
"How would you receive them?"
I don't know
That's the Miracle Engineer's Another Miracle.